SLOTH LIFE

By Wendy Williams

No part of this publication may be reproduced without written permission of the publisher.

First Edition 2023
Printed in the United Kingdom.
ISBN: 978-1-9111511-7-3

© All Aboard Learning 2022
All Aboard Learning Ltd, 267 Banbury Road, Oxford OX2 7HT, UK
AllAboardLearning.com
This book is compatible with All Aboard Phonics UK Editions.

All Aboard Phonics Phase 5
Unit 1 Week 5

Week 1	ay, ou, ie, ea, Mr, Mrs, Ms
Week 2	oy, ir, ue, aw, there, people, oh, their
Week 3	wh, ew, oe, looked, asked, called
Week 4	au, ey, i_e, o_e, could, should, would
Week 5	a_e, u_e, e_e, ph
Week 6	Assessment week

All Aboard Phonics decodable books have a carefully controlled vocabulary and are specifically designed for children who are learning to read and write with All Aboard Phonics, or beginner readers learning at home.

Please take a moment to revise what phoneme (sound) is normally represented by each of these graphemes (letters). It is fine to help the learner if they are not sure.

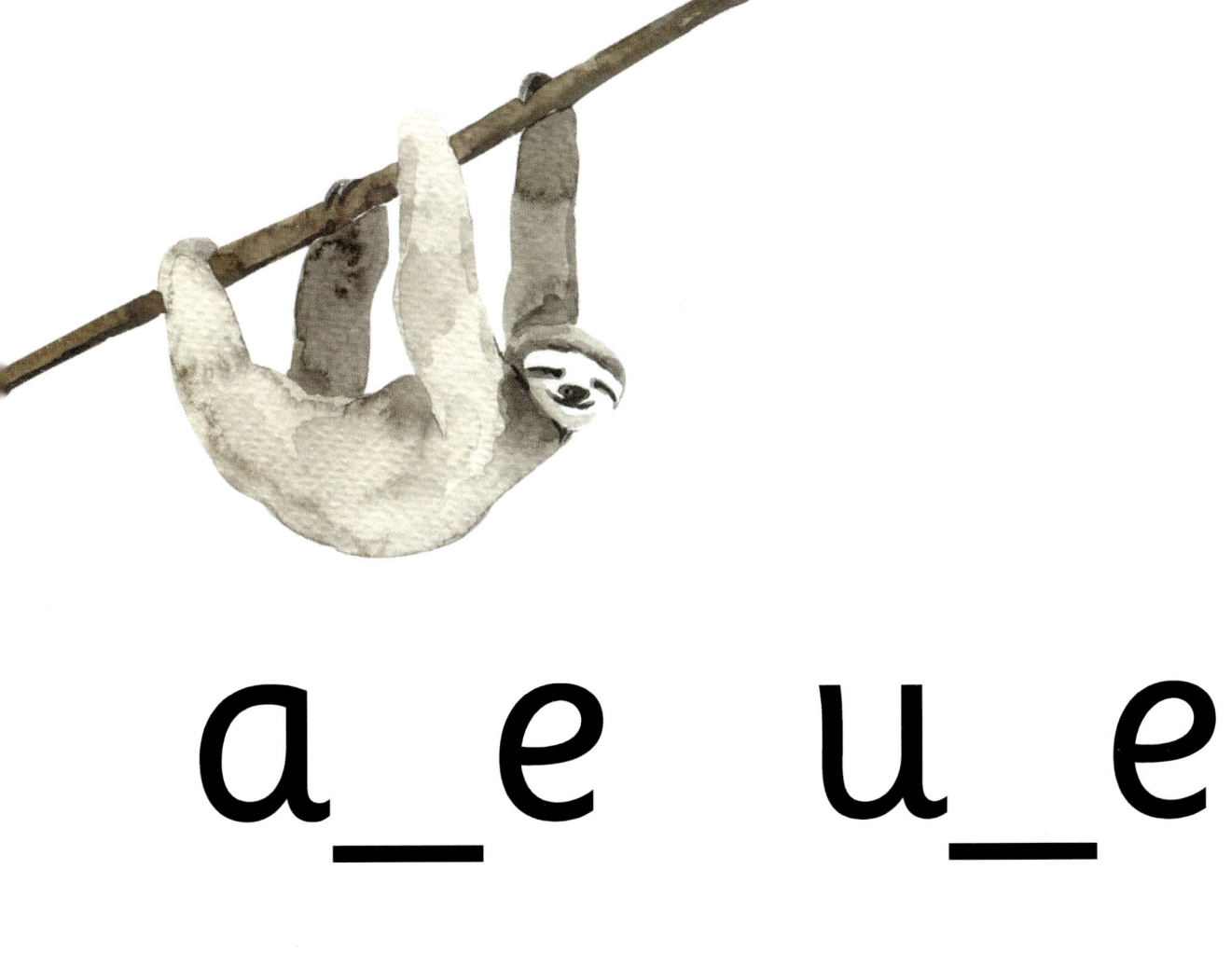

a_e u_e

e_e ph

Sloths are the size of a big cat.

Their coat is made of thick fur.

Bugs crawl in their fur. They are a perfect snack for a sloth!

They hang upside down in trees all day.

They cling to the trees with their three toes.

A sloth can sleep and even eat upside down.

Sloth kids are born upside down too!

The kids do not get hurt if they drop out of a tree.

In fact, they slip off a few times a week!

Sloths eat twigs and buds.

Sloths poo one time per week... but it is a big one.

They have a poo jig that they do.

Then they dig a hole to clean up. How neat!

Sloths are much stronger than people.

You could never yank a sloth from his tree!

They prefer night as they cannot see well in bright light.

I think sloths are cute - do you?

Guided Reading Prompts

Comprehension Questions:
1. How big is a sloth? What is it the size of?
2. What do sloths like to eat?
3. How many toes do they have?
4. Which time of day do sloths like best?

Making Connections:
1. Would you like to meet a sloth? Why or why not?
2. Would you like to be a sloth? Why or why not?
3. If you were going to write a book about an animal, which animal would you choose?

Bonus Activities:
1. Find one word for each of teoday's graphemes in this book. Write it down in a brown sloth-coloured pencil or crayon.
2. Draw a picture of a sloth and name your sloth!
3. With an adult, watch a YouTube video about sloths. What do you notice about how they move?

Photography Credits:

Illustration 1: Canva stock imagery

Photo 1: Photo 116009178 / Sloth © Jonathan Ross | Dreamstime.com

Photo 2: Photo 40590660 / Sloth © Jenhuang99 | Dreamstime.com

Photo 3: Photo 75486069 / Sloth © Kungverylucky | Dreamstime.com

Photo 4: Photo 473416027 / Baby Sloth © Kristel Segeren | Shutterstock.com

Photo 5: Photo 87865052 / Sloth © Raisin7036 | Dreamstime.com

Photo 6: Photo 167025555 © Christoph Lischetzki | Dreamstime.com

Photo 7: Sloth © Mark Kostich from Getty Images Signature via Canva

Photo 8: Photo 25417470 / Sloth © Natakuzmina | Dreamstime.com

Photo 9: Photo 40012298 / Sloth © Misad | Dreamstime.com

Photo 10: Photo 21831373 / Sloth © Seadam | Dreamstime.com

Photo 11: Photo 66676405 / Sloth © Ssh | Dreamstime.com

Photo 12: Photo 181339727 / Sloth © Wirestock | Dreamstime.com

Photo 13: Photo 21661659 / Sloth © Art2eatwith | Dreamstime.com

Photo 14: Photo 33131148 / Sloth © Anekoho | Dreamstime.com

Photo 15: Photo 155552353 © Chrismrabe | Dreamstime.com

Photo 16/Cover Image: Photo 49063562 / Sloth © Janossygergely | Dreamstime.com